Little People, BIG DREAMS®
MIKAELA SHIFFRIN

Written by
Maria Isabel Sánchez Vegara

Illustrated by
Anastasia Ryzhkova

Frances Lincoln
Children's Books

Little Mikaela grew up under a snowy mountain in Colorado, USA. Her parents had her practise skiing as soon as she could walk. At two, she was almost gliding by herself, determined to catch her big brother, Taylor!

It wasn't long before she got her first racing suit. Mikaela even wore it to bed! But she truly fell in love with skiing when she was six. She started training for slalom, a contest where racers zoom downhill while weaving around colourful poles.

'Always Be Faster Than the Boys!' That's what a famous skier wrote on a poster for Mikaela. She loved it so much that when she started racing, she put the letters ABFTTB on her helmet – one for each word on the poster.

Mikaela went to a top school for skiing. She earned many junior titles, including one at an important event in Italy. But her dad taught her that no matter what she achieved, being smart, thoughtful and kind made her a true winner.

At fifteen, Mikaela's mum, Eileen, became her coach. She was also her best friend and travel buddy. Together, they drove across Europe for competitions, while her dad, Jeff, took care of things at home. They were Team Shiffrin!

Between competitions, Mikaela would ride down the slopes, training until her toes were almost frozen. All her hard work paid off in two fleeting minutes of a big night race, when she won her first World Cup. She was just seventeen.

Soon after, she won the Snow Queen competition. Wearing the fairy-tale crown was an honour! Mikaela felt shy about being the centre of attention, but she had to get used to it quickly. She finished the season as the top slalom skier.

For the next seven years, Mikaela broke many records and won lots of World Championship races. She also earned two Olympic gold medals: one in Russia and one in South Korea.

Her ninety-two-year-old nana was one of her biggest fans, tuning in no matter how late it was!

Each season saw Mikaela crowned as the best skier, and it seemed like her reign would never end. But her world turned upside down when her father had a terrible accident and died. She didn't even want to ski anymore.

When she felt ready to come back, Mikaela put her dad's words on her helmet, to always remember him. After a tough time at her third Olympics, some wondered if she was as good as before – but she showed she was even better!

Once she had recovered from a terrifying crash, Mikaela weaved into history again with her 100th World Cup victory. At just twenty-nine, she was the skier with the most wins ever. Yet she knew her journey wasn't just about trophies.

Hoping to help others enjoy the snow as much as she did, Mikaela teamed up with the Share Winter Foundation. Their goal was to make skiing and snowboarding easier for more kids to try, especially those whose families couldn't afford it.

And to this day, little Mikaela – one of the greatest skiers of all time – keeps inspiring the next generation not just to win, but to succeed in the most exciting adventure: living a life that you love.

MIKAELA SHIFFRIN

(Born 1995)

2017

2021

Mikaela Shiffrin was born in Colorado, USA. Her parents were former ski racers, and soon Mikaela's passion for the sport blossomed, too. From an early age, she loved zooming down snowy slopes alongside her older brother. By the age of six, she was already training for slalom, a downhill skiing race. It wasn't long before Mikaela's talents became clear to everyone around her. Over the next few years Mikaela trained hard, entered competitions worldwide and quickly rose to the top of her sport. In 2011, two days before her sixteenth birthday, Mikaela made her World Cup debut, and the following year she won her first victory in that competition. At age eighteen, she became the youngest Olympic slalom champion in history. Her rise to the top continued when she won seventeen

2023

2025

of the World Cup races she entered between 2018 and 2019, setting a record for the most wins in a single season. But when Mikaela's father unexpectedly died, she was overcome with grief and couldn't face competing. Once she was ready, she wowed the world by winning four medals at the World Championships. By 2023, she had won fourteen World Championship medals – the most of any alpine skier in modern history. In 2024, Mikaela suffered an injury during a race that seriously affected her mental health. She took time out to heal, but less than a month after her return, she claimed her 100th World Cup win! Mikaela's amazing achievements show the world that, as well as talent, an athlete needs to have heart, determination and resilience.

Want to find out more about **Mikaela Shiffrin**?
Have a read of this great book:

Mikaela Shiffrin by Joe Tischler

With love to Aven, Reid, Amber, Arthur and their amazing grandma.

Text © 2026 Maria Isabel Sánchez Vegara. Illustrations © 2026 Anastasia Ryzhkova.
Original idea of the series by Maria Isabel Sánchez Vegara, published by Alba Editorial, s.l.u.
"Little People, BIG DREAMS" and "Pequeña & Grande" are trademarks of
Alba Editorial s.l.u. and/or Beautifool Couple S.L.

First published in the UK in 2026 by Frances Lincoln Children's Books, an imprint of The Quarto Group.
1 Triptych Place, London, SE1 9SH, United Kingdom. T 020 7700 6700 www.Quarto.com
EEA Representation, WTS Tax d.o.o., Žanova ulica 3, 4000 Kranj, Slovenia. www.wts-tax.si

All rights reserved.
No part of this publication may be reproduced, stored in a retrieval system, or transmitted, in any form,
or by any means, electrical, mechanical, photocopying, recording or otherwise without the prior written
permission of the publisher or a licence permitting restricted copying.

This book is not authorised, licensed or approved by Mikaela Shiffrin.
Any faults are the publisher's who will be happy to rectify for future printings.
A catalogue record for this book is available from the British Library.
ISBN 978-1-80570-154-5
Set in Futura BT.

Published by Peter Marley and Juliet Matthews
Edited by Lucy Menzies · Editorial management by Izzie Hewitt
Designed by Sasha Moxon, Izzy Bowman and Karissa Santos
Production by Robin Boothroyd
Manufactured in Shanghai, China CC092025
1 3 5 7 9 8 6 4 2

Photographic acknowledgements (pages 28-29, from left to right): 1. US skier Mikaela Shiffrin poses with her parents Eileen and Jeff after winning the women's slalom race at the 2017 FIS Alpine World Ski Championships in St Moritz on 18th February, 2017 (Photo by FABRICE COFFRINI/AFP via Getty Images). 2. Mikaela Shiffrin poses on the podium after placing third at the Women's Super G event on 11th February, 2021, during the FIS Alpine World Ski Championships in Cortina d'Ampezzo, Italian Alps. (Photo by FRANCOIS-XAVIER MARIT/AFP via Getty Images). 3. Mikaela Shiffrin of Team United States celebrates during the Audi FIS Alpine Ski World Cup Women's Giant Slalom on 28th December, 2023, in Lienz, Austria. (Photo by Millo Moravski/Agence Zoom/Getty Images). 4. Mikaela Shiffrin of USA celebrates first place during the award ceremony for Slalom 2nd Run of Audi FIS Ski World Cup Sestriere 2025 on 23rd February, 2025, in Sestriere, Italy. (Photo by Stefano Guidi/Getty Images).

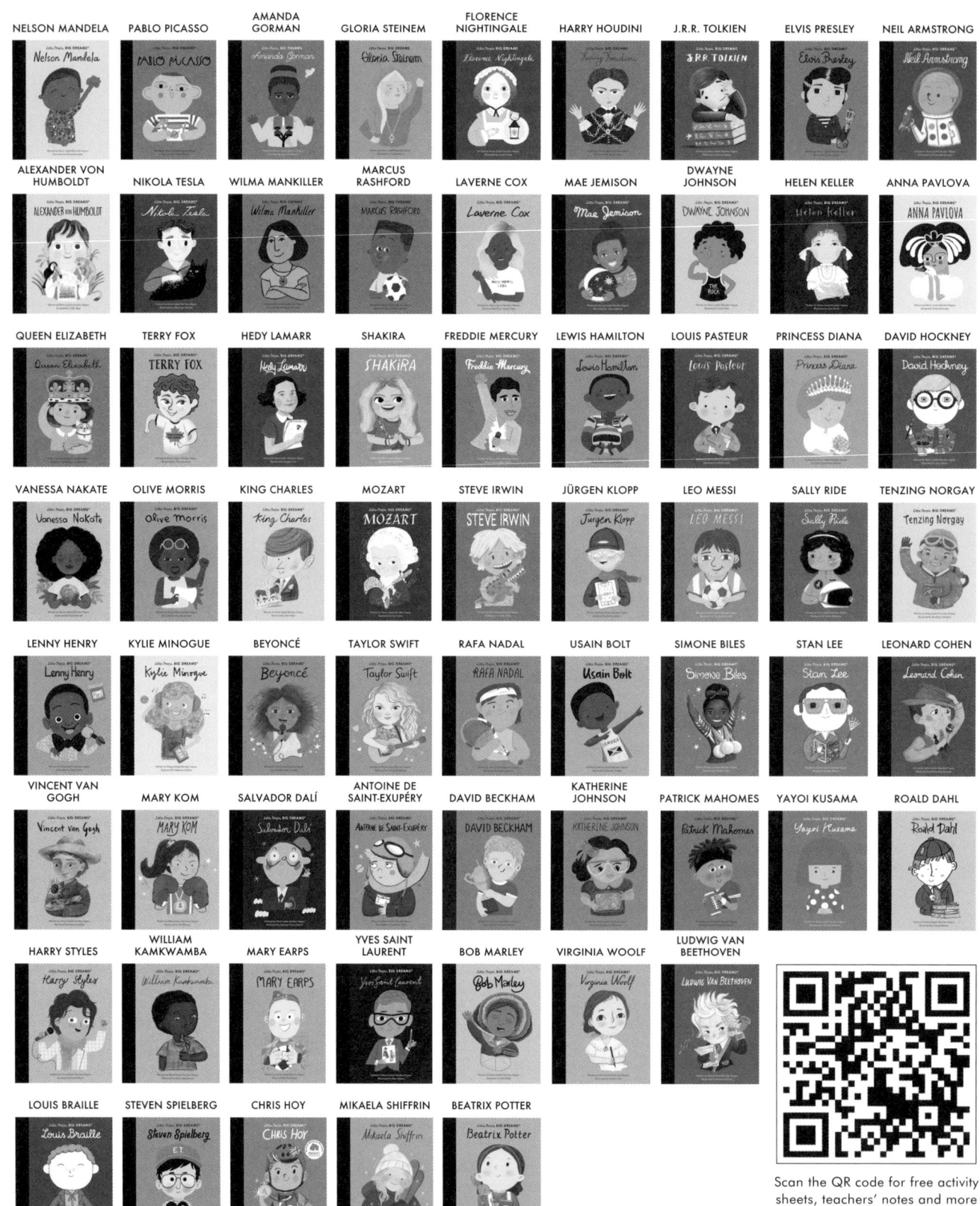

Scan the QR code for free activity sheets, teachers' notes and more information about the series at www.littlepeoplebigdreams.com